GW00642137

March

To

March

Wanney Books

March to March

© 2021 Virginia Kennedy

First published in the United Kingdom in 2021 by Wanney Books

www.wildsofwanney.co.uk

All rights reserved. No part of this book shall be reproduced or transmitted in any form or by any means, electronic or mechanical, including photocopying, recording, or by any information storage and retrieval system without permission in writing from the publisher.

A catalogue record for this book is available from the British Library.

ISBN 978-1-9196249-1-4

Printed by Martins the Printers, TD15 1RS

To all who took the
journey with us

Contents

Introduction

'March to March' records the journey of a group of like-minded people who used a balancing moment in time to pause and turn attention towards meditation and the quiet mind.

Our journey began as a response to the strangeness of the situation of the Covid pandemic lockdown in March 2020. Little did we know it was to last a year. Initially our gathering was a way to retain a sense of community for a small group of yogis and meditators who had met weekly for a class. Then it grew and grew and began a life of its own. New meditators kept finding us until we were a group of 67 in total. Each of us had our own path and landscape, whether it was under a New Zealand sky while sitting on an upturned boat, a garden in Brittany, a school playground in Minneapolis or a woodland in Northumberland. Each of us felt a sense of belonging and companionship.

At first, I was daunted by the task of a daily meditation theme until it dawned on me that if I wrote from my own experience backed up with the Buddhist teachings I have received over the years, that would be good enough.

I had been fortunate to discover Buddhism in India in 1971 first within a lay tradition then through the inspiration of the Theravada Monastic tradition in this country. So, I set about preparing a series of meditations that I would record daily and send in an audio file to those who expressed an interest.

As we came towards the end of this year someone suggested these themes might become a book. So began the journey of distilling from a selection of over 200 recordings a text that could provide both a reminder of these times and something to return to for sustenance. I wanted this to be a team effort, so Lisa, Lynda,

Mary, and I started Zooming and sharing ideas. We began the careful process of selecting, editing, proofreading and reshaping from spoken word to written text.

It seemed a good idea to include some artwork to enrich the book. I approached five members of the group who are artists to offer a painting, which each one generously did, and I made up the number so we could have a piece of art for each month.

Throughout the year, when preparing the meditations, I returned many times to the idea that our little group had a lot in common with a little bird—the wren. This has given us a theme which you may notice as the wren appears in our story.

So, here is our book of reflection and memories which I hope will be a source of joy and nourishment for all.

Virginia Kennedy
4th May 2021

March

Virginia

Safe Haven

21ˢᵗ March 2020

Today's theme is 'Safe Haven'. Today is the spring equinox so here is a simple meditation to start our process:

> *In times of uncertainty when we are looking for a safe feeling, we can use poised attention to focus and avoid getting swept up in the energy of changing times. It is time to step back into a contemplative state of mind.*

> *We can practise this first with scanning the body, feeling where there may be a tightening or greater intensity, and patiently waiting while the body settles. Keep relaxing, and for this meditation use a simple mantra -- just say to yourself 'So'. Notice when you are being swept up and come back to 'So', begin again and again....Good Luck*

Kindness or Metta

25th March 2020

The theme for today is Kindness or in Pali (the language at the time of the Buddha), Metta. In these exceptional times the emotive currents are all around us. We need an antidote and that is the gentle, undemanding quality of Metta:

Being comfortable is the order of the day as we prepare for Metta meditation. Begin the practice of relaxing your body, stretching, yawning. Sit with your hands in your lap. Focus breath awareness into your hands and feel the natural pulse and vibration of sensation. Try to just let the awareness come together without forcing it. It's fine if it does not. Then add contemplation on the kind acts of hands, the giving without expectation. Appreciate your own kindness.

Send that thought now to others on the front line risking so much to keep us healthy.

You can try feeling the gentle sensation throughout the body like a sparkling cool haze from a mountain waterfall. Cool the mind and relax the body. Just be in the sensation without demand. See what happens....Good Luck

Compassion

26th March 2020

When someone enters a monastic life, they are deliberately putting themselves in a situation of both vulnerability and constriction. These two conditions are a crucible for change. We find ourselves in the current situation not by our own choice, but we can decide to turn it into a spiritual experience. Vulnerability is one of the doors to compassion and being held in a time and space reveals the true nature of reality:

Compassion comes naturally from experience and as a result of truly feeling how much we are all connected. It's the opposite of the 'I'm alright Jack' state of mind. For this meditation you can explore that misunderstanding of who we think we are. This is a very simple but profound exercise to stop the mind creating an identity that will suffer by feeling separated from others.

Sitting and settling into the weight of the body, become grounded. As you settle into the touch and weight of the body in key places--the hips, the hands, shoulders arms--release any tension using an extended breath. Then relax the breath. This is your containment (constriction), the body sitting. When thoughts arise gently say to yourself 'who?'. It stops the mind proliferating and reminds us to question the apparent reality. Go back time and time again to just sitting. At the end of the period of time relax and appreciate your efforts.... Good Luck

April

Anne C

Worldly Winds

2ⁿᵈ April 2020

The theme today is looking closely at what disturbs our natural contentment and you may find it is the effect of what the Buddha described as the 8 worldly winds:

Gain and loss...success and failure...pain and pleasure ...honour and insignificance.... As we sit or go about our everyday activities we have surges of these winds which take us off balance.

Often we want to gain something or feel a loss and the mind moves off its steadiness. It can become disturbed, often deeply. When we meditate, we may experience calm during the session and we think we are good meditators, then the next time the mind is all over the place, so we think we are rubbish meditators. The truth is it's impossible to succeed or fail at meditation. We can look at that hunger for success as our meditation instead. This leads to greater understanding. It's the same with pain and pleasure, fame and insignificance, all the worldly winds. It's a useful way to mature the mind, watching the way it works. One way I found to work for me is to say internally when I recognise the disturbance 'I know you'. Then you wait patiently for the storm to pass.... Good Luck

Intention

There is little guarantee what the future holds but we have a chance to influence it by our intention now. If you like, our aspiration for the day, where we aspire to abide is a lovely way to start the day, the week:

The Vietnamese Zen Master and poet Thich Nhat Hanh had a way to bring our intention down to one breath 'I breathe in, I calm the body; I breathe out, I smile.' Smiling can relax us and our attitude toward others.

I find it good to keep it simple when thinking of a good intention for the day. Here's one …. Train myself to be at ease with life and easy to live with. Be like a shrub, able to flourish anywhere, not a hot-house plant needing special conditions all the time.

So, with the best of intentions, I offer you: 'Breathe in, calm the body; breathe out, smile'…. Good Luck

Balance

31st April 2020

Today's theme is the balance of energy. Wouldn't it be wonderful if we all kept this balance in our lives?

Music which is harmonious brings contentment to the listener. This comes about when members of the orchestra or choir balance their efforts, making a melodic sound.

> *If you learn an instrument or train to perform a skill it takes a lot of practice. Most of us try too hard, tighten the strings too tight. I learnt this mostly through yoga. Here the body teaches you all the time. It's good to learn to make friends with our body, not battle with it. Balance is a good example of this: if you try too hard you fall over, if you try too little you fall over. It's that 'Goldilocks' moment, to be just right…. Good Luck*

May

Catriona

Everything Teaches Us

14th May 2020

At times it is good to go back to basics, just sitting with the breath, feeling it in the body and waiting without expectation:

Doing less is often more. Not even trying to meditate, just sitting somewhere and relaxing into the breath can be calming.

Sit in a way that supports the back and allows you to settle into the body. Start with 5 slowing down breaths, extending the out breath consciously. You can use the thought "breathing in with ease and breathing out with a smile."

Gradually let the breath take you to just sitting. Allow the body to feel heavy. Let go of the breath as a sigh. There's just this, nothing more. See what it teaches you...no expectation, just calming and gladdening the mind.... Good Luck

June

Virginia

Relative Time

Time is a strange thing. It can lengthen or shorten in accordance with our occupation, mood, emotional state or how we imagine things to be. It is greatly affected by the perception of pressure! So, if we allow ourselves time can we feel spaciousness?

The more sense of urgency we feel, the more compressed our world seems to become. Some of you are under great pressure and running important systems for us all. It is all too familiar to feel the pressure of a list that must be completed. We have all done it and know sometimes we just have to 'lean into' time to get things done. But we are interested in balance in this practice of meditation. So, a capacity to feel spaciousness has a great benefit to our well-being.

Overwhelmed by rushing, we are compressed. Why not open the doors, let the air in, feel the wind and let the sun warm our hearts? Stop, breathe, wait and listen. Be on the edge of time and see what happens…. Good Luck

Compassion for Ourselves

16ᵗʰ June 2020

As we notice the way our mind works, we become aware of the effect of our thinking on our ability to be relaxed both in company and on our own. Meditation can be very enjoyable when we practice self-worth and compassion:

> *The opposite of valuing and appreciating who we are is self-pity. When we feel sorry for ourselves we tighten up physically. Our world becomes more limited. We can even feel the throat tightening as we knot ourselves. The change comes when we relax and accept who we are and the situation right now. Understanding and compassion for ourselves can replace self-pity. One leads to suffering, the other to freedom.*

> *When you sit, be aware of the body, physically relax. Send a warm soothing breath into each part of the body. Relax into the hips, feel the hands open and accepting, drop the shoulders, unfurrow the brow and breathe, remaining calm in the present. This is the true self--it is refreshing and feeds our ability to understand and have compassion…. Good Luck*

July

Anne C

Gratitude

9th July 2020

The theme is gratitude for our body and mind which serve us so loyally. When we come to look at the nature of our body, we make some assumptions which we rarely question:

We expect a lot of our body. We wish to go somewhere and our feet take us; we eat something and our taste buds give us pleasure; we open our eyes and see colour, beautiful patterns, our friends and family. There isn't a bone, sinew, or muscle in our body that hasn't over the years worked very hard to satisfy our demands. Granted we wash it, clothe it, make sure it is fed and watered, maybe pamper it with comforts, but have we ever said 'thank you'? We forget to do this because we go on the assumption it is 'ours'. It is our slave! Then when it plays up or gets out of sorts, at best we stop and take note but maybe not even then.

One way I have found to counterbalance this neglect is to stop, relax and take individual parts of the body and thank each part for its wonderful service. Take a few minutes to do this, lying down or sitting. Use the breath and relaxation techniques to visit part by part and say thank you…. Good Luck

Feelings and Perceptions

30th July 2020

Our experiences are coloured by our feelings and perceptions and this can change radically when we concentrate the mind and our true nature is revealed:

Every day we have many feelings. Sometimes we are happy, sometimes sorrowful, sometimes angry, irritated or afraid, and these feelings fill our mind and heart. It's like stringing a necklace: when we are hurt, we thread all the moments of hurt we stored. It's the same for all the emotions; when we feel grief, all the losses in our life are put on the same thread. This is compounded feeling. But this can change and our perspective can too.

When we meditate we become aware of these feelings but can observe them from a distance. Otherwise we get caught up in the feelings—we all do, it's who we are. When we meditate we learn from these feelings, and what we learn can change our perception of these feelings.

It's like a house we are sorting out. Every room has boxes full of what we once treasured. We have to move on so there is a massive sort out. Some things are easy to let go of, while others we linger over. We have to do the sorting or we will forever be tripping over those boxes. Having selected what is important to us, we can let the rest go and it feels great…. Good Luck

August

Virginia

Doing Nothing

7th August 2020

We don't always need to be productive, but living in a society fixated on getting things done can leave us feeling we are judged by the level of our activity:

Celebration of allowing ourselves to just hang out is part of the notion of 'letting go'. Unless we allow a little space, how can we notice the present?

There are four ways we can 'let go'.

The first is to let go of the past. It's a prison with an open door. In it are all manner of memories, grievances, disappointments and joys never to be repeated. Just accept that fact and don't rehash past experiences all over again. Do nothing with memory.

The second is to let go of the future. We have absolutely no idea what this will be, and it is only in the present we can do something about the future.

The third is let go of the complaining, fault-finding mind...'It's not fair!' We know we get a mixture of experiences, some good, some not so good--no need to let either bother us.

The fourth is let go of expectation of rewards for our good actions and be generous in the present.

This way of doing nothing can be exhilarating and certainly frees up time.... Good Luck

Heedless Speech

12th August 2020

When we realise the impact of our words and actions on our state of mind it is wise to consider that interrelationship. We can begin to work on 'sila' or moral action through our meditation:

We see the need to match the way we speak with our good intentions. But speech is full of habits and slips into all manner of unfortunate pitfalls. It is well recognized as one of the hardest precepts, but small changes can make us match our intensions with our speech. Malicious gossip that is motivated by a wish to put someone down and elevate ourselves is wrong speech. To practice right speech asks would you have the same conversation if the person were present? Have you ever found yourself 'topping' someone with an even bigger, greater, or worse experience which immediately belittles what they have offered? Being open and honest is so refreshing, but if it would be used to make someone feel vulnerable it is worth being quiet.

How often have we listened to people in powerful positions being defensive, unable to be open and admit what they know or genuinely say 'sorry'? What a different world we would have! I could go on but in the interest of moderation I will spare you and wish you, wish all of us, well with this noble task…. Good Luck

September

Virginia

The Company We Keep

2nd September 2020

In our concern for our own and others' happiness and creating peace in our world the first guidance from The Buddha was about the company we keep:

You start to see how easily influenced we can be, even when we feel ourselves stable. As we proceed on our path we really want to associate with wise people. We chose our friends carefully and value them more and more as we come to see things differently through meditation.

Part of the richness of the practice we are exploring is the open-minded curiosity and interest in a bigger picture. So, we gravitate towards like-minded people. We are not fooled by the attraction of a 'colourful character' who may entertain us but not sustain us. One of the joys of a good friend is the fact that they not only know us for who we are and appreciate us, but they know themselves.

In such a relationship everyone is starting from an understanding, an honesty and wish to move towards a place where the balance is just right. No point-scoring or jealousies, sympathy-hunting or one-upmanship, just honest warmth and a good heart.

Associating with wise friends is the highest blessing.... Good Luck

Beauty

Beauty brings us back to a state of vulnerability, innocence and abandonment. We can witness wonders and marvels that put us in touch with nature:

Beauty can be a spectacular glow of a sunset, the delight in a child's face, the joy of bright colours and in the words of a poem. It can also be the acknowledgement and expression of a feeling, the logical process of thinking, the discovery of truth, in the realization of harmony and the absence of fear.

We need beauty and need to be able to recognise it wherever we see it. It is the essence of life. Its presence pushes the artist to create, opens the heart, leads the brain to clarity, invites the mind to comprehend and brings the body to participate.

You can find yourself unexpectedly absorbed by beauty any time and any place…. Good Luck

Inspired Self-Interest

29th September 2020

Selflessness is overrated. We well-brought-up souls have been trained to think a life well spent means only helping others. The truth is we can get kindness tangled up with issues closer to guilt:

There could be a different way to look at generosity. If we feel we 'should' be doing more for others it is a clue as to where our motives dwell; the irony is that we don't serve anyone else by suppressing our true passions anyway. More often than not, by doing what you really enjoy you kindle a fire that helps to keep the rest of us warm.

When you give spontaneously, or in response to a heartfelt concern for someone else, then the energy is very different and so too are the results…. Good Luck

October

Jane

Biased Thinking

14th October 2020

We mostly experience life with a biased mind. Experience is highly valued, but it can also take us into a narrow channel, a biased view on what is happening:

Creating generalizations is a shorthand way to live. We do it to save time, to make sense of our world, but often we are putting people in boxes, which means we are putting ourselves in one as well.

For example, how often do we let our attention wholly focus on what people are saying? We think we get it, but our attention is only taking in a small fraction of what is being said. If we want to open ourselves to a fresh and fuller experience of life we could start with just this: listening and really looking at what others are trying to say…. Good Luck

Feet on the Ground

21ˢᵗ October 2020

There is a common trait, when an impressionable mind first encounters meditation, to become full of ardour and embarrassingly grand utterances. Fortunately, this trait is curable! When we can come down to earth with our feet on the ground it is such a relief:

I first took up with meditation in the rarefied setting of the foothills of the Himalayas. It was heady stuff. I came 'down to earth' and found my 'feet on the ground' flying into Belfast, my hometown, in May 1972--not its finest hour. It's a bit of a trampoline reaction. Meditation can make us extra sensitive and a bit precious as we experience the unhooking of fixed views.

This is when I found the effect of the physical aspects of yoga and also physical work quite a relief. It's a constant balancing act, but at the heart of being well-grounded is not taking ourselves too seriously.

This is when I learned you never succeed at meditation nor do you fail. It is just something you do.... Good Luck

November

Virginia

Enlightenment

18th November 2020

It's no surprise that the word 'light' is part of Enlightenment. It is possibly a key to lessening the burden and putting down new foundations which are based in hope:

When we open the Pandora's box of our apparent reality, out fly into the light all the woes we have harboured in our subconscious. They now are in the light and with them is hope. This could mean 'enlightenment' or 'waking up', to gain insights on all manner of things in our world, including the realization we don't need to hold on with a precious ownership to all the thoughts and feelings we had locked in the mind.

Those thoughts and feelings can be very mischievous when they are in the box of our subconscious. When we first meditate it can be quite a roller coaster as we honestly look at these. It's not an 'airy fairy' practice, that's for sure!

However, we can bring 'lightness' to this. In the Egyptian myth of Duat (the underworld) the hearts of the dead are weighed against a single feather. The weighing scales are honesty. If the heart is lighter than an ostrich feather on the scales of truth the owner goes to heaven. So, being honest makes us 'light as a feather'.... Good Luck

Lighting Our Own Lamp

25th November 2020

How to resist pressure and the prison of conformity with the burden to meet other people's ideas and standards:

It all adds up to pressure. Towards the end of Buddha's life when he was aged 80 years, after 45 years spent teaching, many of his followers would have relied solely on him for inspiration. Yet the Buddha encouraged us to experience and evaluate his teachings for ourselves. He was clear about this. If we want to be free from suffering, we need to light our own lamps. It's a lovely image: the light, warmth and focus that come when we turn to ourselves.

There is a lot of conditioning that can bring pressure on us and stress to meet everyone's expectations. But if we stop, light our lamps, and see what we are doing, we can be a lot freer.... Good Luck

The Lesson of Fire

26th November 2020

Fire is a powerful force in nature and a central theme at this time of year. We gather around fires for comfort, for a feeling of belonging and safety:

This is not the only nature of fire. Fire is a powerful and unpredictable force of nature. It is one of the 4 elements we are made up of, a magical and consuming energy. It is the stuff of alchemy. Early civilizations worshipped fire for these properties.

At the time of the Buddha there was a sect of Fire Worshippers who came to him for teaching. He delivered a sermon that became known as the Fire Sermon. It was, in modern parlance, a game changer. He turned the request into a profound teaching on the nature of our suffering. He looked at our senses as if they were on fire, burning with aversion and delusions of ownership.

We have desire to consume experience and crave more and more, but with enough insight, we can sidestep this process. When we see clearly we don't have to follow blindly. We can rest, relax and appreciate what we have right now, nothing more.... Good Luck

December

Sheila

Being True to Ourselves

Today's theme is being true to ourselves. Understanding brings about peaceful states of mind as we relax and accept things as they are:

I used to notice a type of passive-aggressive peaceful pose that seemed to go hand in hand with early enthusiasm for meditation. Retreats I went to in the 70's were awash with drifty 'beautiful' people all trying to pretend they were peaceful. (Ram Dass called this being "phony holy".)

Ironically, it is the ability to accept these states of mind that gives peace. You don't need to change anything, just be yourself and start to be honest.

Self-improvement is another form of agitation for the mind because it suggests we aren't good enough. It took me a long time to realize that I was just exactly where I should be and that changes may come but from insight not from some assumed peaceful pose.

So let us all just for today say it is good enough just as it is.... Good Luck

Unwanted Thoughts

20th December 2020

There is a misconception that by meditating you can get rid of unwanted thoughts and feelings:

What meditation does do is give us a set of skills and tools to be able to stay with unwelcome feelings and thoughts, to give them room so they can defuse their energy naturally.

Here are a couple of ideas. Think of time spent meditating like making a new friendship with our thoughts and feelings. Be totally generous, give space, be open and listen.

Sometimes in a yoga class I use the idea we have borrowed someone else's body to use and want to give it back in a better state. I know it's an odd idea but it works for me…. Good Luck

Home

22nd December 2020

There is such a yearning at this time of year to head home or to create a warm and friendly place. Many struggle with the ideals of what that should be:

It makes me wonder, where did these ideas come from anyway? Some selective memories of childhood or an idealized presentation in other people's homes, a film we once saw, a book we read or even a song could fuel the notions. The ideas are heavily weighted in a mix of tradition, habit, commercial pressures and wishing to impress. Home should be the place of safety, peace and happiness, but how often is that the case?

If we want to feel safe and accepted, it must come down to how we feel about ourselves. If I love one person, I feel at home with that person, and if I love many people, I will feel at home with many. But if I am really bold and learn to love myself, then I can be at home wherever I am in all manner of circumstances.

If we can drop our expectations of perceived perfection, then moment by moment with lots and lots of little easings we can relax to accept life as it is. I am reminded of a quote from Ram Dass: "We're all just walking each other home." If we can come to this realisation we can be at peace....
Good Luck

January

Virginia

Aspiration

5th January 2021

There is a tradition within the Buddhist practice of clearing the way for the New Year, first by forgiving yourself and others for any real or imagined hurt, then taking on an aspiration for the new year ahead. Mine is 'lightness':

I would like to invite you to join me in looking for opportunity to bring lightness into our lives and the lives of others. This may be a modest act of joyful giving; lightness suggests qualities which aren't demanding. You are not trying to make things turn out the way you want but to know and understand your circumstance as it is.

Lightness may mean shedding light on our habits of thought, seeing how a sound, sight or even smell can trigger a memory and how one thought leads to another. You may see how memory triggers emotion and how this can affect moods. By shedding light on these habits, we are bringing inner light to our lives.

We could light a candle and stop for a moment to think about the light in the dark. We can after all only shine when there is dark. So, let's lightly dust the problems from our shoulders, know them for what they are, and bring a light touch to our meditation.

This is an aspiration, something to move towards, not a resolution which requires a lot of will power and hence a heavier approach. Lightness doesn't need to succeed, it just is.... Good Luck

Direct Experience

12th January 2021

Meditation offers us a direct experience which can give us a refuge for the heart. It's a steadying experience which allows the rip tides of the mind to pass and leave us steadier, calmer and happier:

> *The image which is sometimes used to reflect on the nature of meditation is a lotus flower. It has been used as a focus for meditation in different religions and Tibetan Buddhism has a chant to go with the image. The translation from the Sanskrit is:*

> *'The impure body, speech and mind are transformed through kindness and wisdom to the jewel in the heart of the lotus "compassion".'*

> *The lotus grows out of a muddy lake and opens its petals one after another as the heat of the sun reveals the lotus' true heart, which is pure. The outer petals may be a bit bruised and discoloured but once the sun's rays have opened the outer petals, the next layer of petals opens until the pure heart is warmed by the sun. It is a perfect analogy for meditation. When conditions of warmth and receptivity are there the heart will relax. We can have a direct experience of body and mind and become open to compassionate awareness inside and out.*

> *We are not responsible for this happening. It is not something we do, design or arrange to happen. We are only setting up the conditions with a lightness of attention to the body and mind, creating an agreeable collected state of awareness.*

We just set the time aside from the rip tides of compulsive thoughts, reactions, repetitive patterns, persuasions, emotions and tendencies. These are all where the lotus is rooted in the mud. The water is our capacity to be still and the sun is our warmth and compassionate awareness.

So the suggestion for today is to use this image with or without the meaning or even chant quietly internally to calm the mind. We may just decide to be still and wait, bringing attention back to the body sitting, standing or walking. It's a way to have direct experience of nature.... Good Luck

February

Penny

Letting Go

3rd February 2021

I don't know about you but when I hear the encouragement to "let go" it makes me want to say 'how'? It's not always that easy. Why is this? When we sit still and create a peaceful space to relax into meditation what gets in the way?

There may be repetitive thoughts, habitual worries or just a wish for a different experience. We can come to meditation with great ideals but the truth is it is a very down-to-earth experience. It concerns what is happening right now.

Before we 'let go' we need to understand what lies behind our holding on to thoughts and states of mind. Once we see the desire which is unsettling the mind it is then possible to let go. Without that insight we have no reason to 'let go' so we don't.

The desire may be for a different type of experience. If you are lucky enough to experience a peaceful state when things come and go, 'letting go' is no problem. The problem comes when you want to repeat that experience. Once we see this as desire it is uprooted. The causes of 'holding on' have been uncovered and 'letting go' is the natural result. It just dissolves.... Good Luck

A Lightness of Being

17ᵗʰ February 2021

Meditation offers us an opportunity to reset our relationship with ourselves and our experiences:

My mother used to use the expression when we were getting upset 'making heavy weather of things'. You can feel yourself getting caught by concerns, taking things personally or indulging in self-pity. When we stop and look at the nature of this heavy weather it is all to do with attachment to an idea of how we think life should treat us.

By holding our attention lightly this intensity can dissolve of its own accord. Sometimes just being able to laugh and share with friends can do it. But we can also just sit with our thought and moods until they change, and the mind begins to shine again with happiness. When we want to create a watercolour painting which shines, it is important to leave some space so the light can come through.... Good Luck

Doing Nothing

24th February 2021

For most of our lives the concept of 'doing nothing' was likened to the sin of idleness. Let us reclaim this concept and elevate it to where it truly belongs:

Giving ourselves permission to just do nothing is profoundly peaceful. A sense of relief comes when we are not trying to achieve anything, become somebody, be distracted, or entertain ourselves or others. It is only when we do something as simple as stop, sit down, lie down, or stand still and just be that we realise that peace is present as the background to ordinary life. It requires wisdom to just do nothing. It is beyond just slowing down or relaxing. We are making peace with passing thoughts. To take yourself into this space, relax into the out breath and trust yourself.

Once you find this escape hatch from the 'becoming mind' you will be able to unlock it any time you want. There is still plenty of time to do everything else in the day, but it just feels a whole lot lighter when you know how to do nothing really well. If someone asks what you are doing, say 'nothing and I haven't finished yet'…. Good Luck

March

Anne C

Managing Expectations

9th March 2021

It is almost a year since we were required to radically change our expectations of what we could do. Now new possibilities are opening up, but this can be a problem for some of us:

As we sense the energy of suppressed anticipation around us, it is hard not to give way to overwhelming prospects. It is important that we be able to manage our expectations. To prepare for this, let's return to meditation as training and for understanding.

Even in quiet times we are capable of over-expectation. We can easily treat mindfulness as an answer to everything and feel disappointed when we find there are still times when we are troubled. We look for peace and see a mind brimming with thoughts. Misguidedly we imagine the goal of meditation is a spacious calm mind. It is quite possible to use it as an escape instead of a technique to learn how to manage our expectations through understanding and gentleness.

*Peace comes from acceptance and compassion for every thought, every mood and shift in circumstance. It takes time and a gentle, subtle practice: 10 minutes a day to train ourselves in not **looking** for happiness but **recognising** happiness..... Good Luck*

Integrated Practice

10ᵗʰ March 2021

This week we have been looking at our relationship with meditation. Today we are focusing on integrating practice into everyday life:

It is a strange thing that in this practice the amount of time we devote to formal practice does not always bring about the most peace of mind.

It is the quality of attention and the relationship with our own thoughts and feelings that matter. Establishing a compassionate approach and choosing this as a reason for meditation changes the way we experience this time. With the 10 minutes we set aside to develop mindfulness we can celebrate every moment we feel present. We train ourselves by gently coming back to the breath and being present.

Then during the day we take lots and lots of moments to pause and be aware of touch, the breath and other senses. By integrating this connection with attention and action we truly feel the benefits of the training. This is not an esoteric, other-worldly practice but one that gives us more control of our own responses. This in turn gives greater freedom.... Good Luck

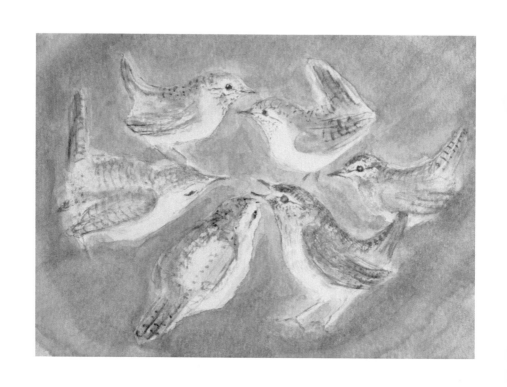

Virginia

A Chime of Wrens

It has been a source of joy to me over this past year to watch our group grow as like-minded people coming together. It reminds me of a chime of wrens:

Wrens are normally solitary and very independent birds, but when they are under stress from adverse weather they seek each other out. They come together as a 'chime' in one place, huddling with their heads pointing together to offer heat, support and shelter. I like the idea we have sheltered with our heads together, pointing towards reflective qualities as the world around us becomes quite unrecognisable.

Coming together in this way we are reminding each other of the value of being at ease with what is happening. We gain confidence and encouragement knowing we are sharing something quite unique. We still engage in quite different lives with differing experiences. This is the richness of an open-minded group who chose to support each other. I am so grateful for our shared interest over this past year.

Our Story

Some thoughts from meditators

In March 2020 my flight home from New Zealand was cancelled and my world changed to one of loneliness and isolation. To cope with each day I would walk to a tiny, secluded beach where I lay on an upturned boat and stared up into the trees. There, I would listen to the calm, wise words of my friend Virginia, accompanied by the beautiful birdsong of a Tui. My sense of isolation disappeared in place of peace, love and wisdom.

I no longer have the beach but I still have those words.

– Anne C

I would never have envisaged all the 6.30's we have been blessed with and the bonus is we can scroll right the way back and still listen again and again and hear that 'GOOD LUCK' which has sustained me not only at 6.30 a.m. but I pick them up throughout the day and night at work and at home, through busy days, joyful days, worrying times and stressful times--it has been and will continue to be so many immeasurable blessings.

– Anne P

After working at the building society for over 20 years I found myself in a position of becoming the manager in the year of the pandemic. I kept my own life on track by placing an even greater focus on my meditation practice. I meditate daily; I attended my lovely zoom meditation evenings and days which were always my 'tablet of stone'.

– Verena

As a nurse my career has taken many paths, and at the beginning of the pandemic my path took me to intensive care. As I drove to work I knew that I had to prepare for what the day would bring and the daily "ting" announcing the arrival of Virginia's meditation was a huge part of my preparation to go in. After a few minutes sitting in the carpark, listening to the theme of the day, I was ready. Throughout the day when times were tough Virginia's voice would return in my head, like a hand of support on my shoulder.

– Amanda

To hear the wisdom of the Buddhist way Virginia described as gentle holding of awareness without grasping. My own religious background comes from what was also originally called 'The Way'. This light of awareness shines within and beyond the borders of our traditions. It brings the realization that everything is interconnected. Everything is made 'whole' again, healed again.

– Pete

Longframlington yoga group started on WhatsApp at the Spring Equinox 2020 and we were all at a loss due to the Pandemic. That first meditation was followed by very many more and having yoga on zoom meant we were all safe and all as one again.

I looked forward to both and I do not doubt that meditations have given me a tool to get through anxieties and difficulties. The best ones free the mind, giving space for a fresh perspective to the situation. I became more mindful but when in doubt I breathe in-refresh; breath out-relax and Smile.

– Ruth

17th March 2020... A quick decision - I got on the last ferry from Portsmouth to France - lockdown in the UK was about to happen - was I running away or racing towards a new episode in my life?

I thought I'd be away a couple of weeks. The next five months were filled with sunshine. But the empty streets, long queues for delicious French bread, Gendarmes checking ID and reasons for being out of the house, made it feel like a strange wartime atmosphere. A time of dislocation, uncertainty, sometimes fear. However, every morning I received a short, gentle message. An idea, a suggestion, a ribbon of thought between me and my friends in England. Virginia had found a way to hold us kindly in our meditation connection, a support and a link to the familiar.

17th March 2021... Back home in England, content, lucky, healthy, a thousand memories of an extraordinary year and still listening to those uplifting and gentle messages!

– Jean

What a year it's been, with so much to disorientate and unsettle both body and mind, reminding us all of our frailty and mortality .... But not entirely! From this sometimes very grey cloud have come regular flashes of light, wisdom, compassion and good humour. For twelve months regular and fresh contemplations have arrived without fail, which, even for a 'seasoned' meditator, have proved a real blessing, grounding, encouraging, reassuring and thought provoking. A lovely blend of Dhamma, common sense and good humour. Meditation/contemplation can sometimes seem, rightly in some ways, an awfully Serious and Significant practice, but it is the lightness of touch of these contemplations, and the generosity of spirit with which they are offered, that have made them so accessible and endearing, a sort of 'spiritual' vaccination against the fears and anxieties of the current 'zeitgeist'. Good luck, indeed!

– Angie

Working with and leading a bunch of youngish lads through lockdown has shown me clearly their concerns and anxieties are just as real as anyone else's is of our generation, simply expressed differently. Listening in to Virginia's daily offering has been so helpful to be reminded of our true allies in uncertain times. Actively promoting honesty for what I don't know, reflecting respect for all manner of responses and especially attentiveness to their silence has been crucial to working through the weeks and finding a level ease for cheerfulness to emerge.

– Geoff

I have come to meditation late in life, with a scant knowledge of the thoughts and sayings of the Buddha. Your daily WhatsApp meditations have been a revelation and, along with reading several books on the subject, have been a valuable introduction to the practice. As you have insisted, this is not a competition and not to expect to become an 'expert' overnight. However, your topics and kindly words have inspired me to 'have ago', so thank you so much.

– Nigel

Aside from enjoying the thought-provoking meditations which have encouraged me to view familiar issues from new perspectives, I have found great pleasure and comfort in the way the groups of quite disparate people have come together with a sense of shared purpose.

– Carol

After years of living in San Francisco and attempts at meditation I finally began a regular practice a distance over 6,000 miles as Virginia and her friendly group welcomed me.

At a time of great global upheaval, the idea that Virginia and these participants were also dealing with the pandemic, and its attendant issues, lent me a sense of connection which enabled me to step out of my comfort zone and into a virtual meditation practice in a small town in the North of England.

I am grateful to be a part of this group

May we all continue to grow in our practice.

– Delores

Acknowledgements

The making of this book has had its own journey and without the friendship, generosity and talent of members of our group it would never have come to be.

I wish, with heartfelt gratitude, to thank Mary Carter, Lisa Heinrich and Lynda Humble who helped me select and edit the years' worth of recordings into this collection.

I wanted the book to be more than just words. Nature has sustained and nurtured us at every stage so a special thank you to the artists who have generously shared their art Anne Curtis, Jane Akhurst, Penny Wakefield-Pearce, Catriona Jennings and Sheila Maurice.

We were fortunate to have Ian Hall as our Publisher and Ivor Rackham as our photographer.

Finally to the fine tradition of meditation teachers who have offered me inspiration over the years

Virginia